Weekly Reader Books presents

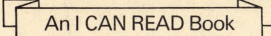

An I CAN READ Book

OOTAH'S LUCKY DAY

by Peggy Parish

Pictures by Mamoru Funai

HARPER & ROW, PUBLISHERS

New York, Evanston, and London

For Lane and Margaret Smith,
with love

OOTAH'S LUCKY DAY
Text copyright © 1970 by Margaret Parish
Pictures copyright © 1970 by Mamoru Funai
All rights reserved. No part of this book may be used or reproduced in any
manner whatsoever without written permission except in the case of brief
quotations embodied in critical articles and reviews. Printed in the United
States of America. For information address Harper & Row, Publishers, Inc.,
49 East 33rd Street, New York, N. Y. 10016. Published simultaneously in Can-
ada by Fitzhenry & Whiteside Limited, Toronto.
Library of Congress Catalog Card Number: 70-105467

OOTAH'S LUCKY DAY

Ootah awoke very early.

"I am so hungry," he said,

"and it is so cold."

He looked where the fire should be.

There was no oil for the fire.

There was no meat

for the cooking pot.

He said, "Oh,

why didn't the hunters

take me with them!"

Ootah had begged to go.

But his father said

they had no time for boys.

"I could have helped,"

thought Ootah.

"And we need help.

My people are hungry.

We must have meat

or we will have to eat the dogs."

Ootah did not want to eat his dogs.

"I know," he said.

"I will take my dogs.

I will take my sled.

And I will go hunting myself."

Ootah called his dogs.

One by one

he hitched them to his sled.

He took his harpoon and his knife.

And he started out hunting.

"I do not want

my people to starve," he said.

"Oh, let this be my lucky day!"

Ootah's sled

skimmed across the snow.

He looked for animal tracks.

But he saw only the tracks

of his own dogs.

Then Ootah looked toward
the frozen sea.
Far away he saw a black spot.
The spot did not move.

"Maybe it is a seal!" said Ootah.

"Seal meat would taste good.

Seal blubber would make

a warm fire.

Oh, please let it be a seal!"

Ootah drove his sled

onto the ice.

The spot grew bigger and bigger.

"A walrus!

It is a walrus!" said Ootah.

"A walrus is even bigger

than a seal."

He watched the walrus.

It slid back into the water.

Ootah knew just what to do.

He dug a deep narrow hole

in the ice.

He put the end of his harpoon line

into the new hole.

He poured water around the line.

"There," he said.

"The water will freeze.

When I throw my harpoon,

the line will hold tight.

I don't want that walrus to get away."

Then he sat down to wait.

Ootah stayed still. Very still.

The walrus must not see him.

The walrus must not hear him.

Ootah waited and he waited.

He was cold and hungry,

but he did not move.

Suddenly he heard a splash.

He saw a black nose

poke out of the hole.

A wrinkled head followed the nose.

Ootah drew back his harpoon.

He held his breath.

He must wait

for just the right moment.

The walrus pulled more of himself

out of the water.

"Now!" thought Ootah.

22

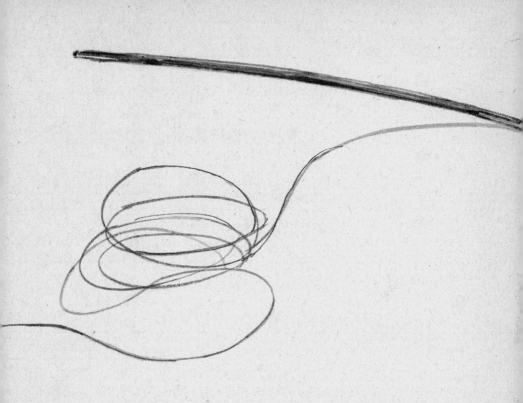

With all his might

he threw that harpoon.

The harpoon hit the walrus.

The walrus flopped over on the ice.

Ootah stared at the big animal.

"I did it!" he whispered.

"I killed a walrus!"

Ootah grinned. "Food!" he shouted.

"Food for everyone,

and oil for our fire!"

The dogs began to bark.

Ootah ran to the sled.

"Let's go!" he shouted.

"Let's get that walrus

and go home."

Ootah brought the sled

close to the walrus.

He tried to get the walrus

onto the sled.

But he could not move it.

He pulled as hard as he could,

but the walrus still did not move.

"Oh, I wish the men

were here," said Ootah.

He could not leave the walrus.

Something might get it.

And his people needed meat.

Ootah tried again and again

to move the walrus.

But he could not do it.

He was tired.

He was so hungry.

He felt like giving up.

Then suddenly the walrus

popped out of the hole.

He landed right on Ootah's sled.

"It must be magic," Ootah whispered.

Then he saw the magic.

Another big walrus!

"One walrus is enough for me!"

he said.

Ootah took off.

The dogs pulled the sled

off the ice.

They stopped and sniffed the air.

"What is it? What is it?" said Ootah.

"Come on, let's go home."

But the dogs began to growl.

Suddenly they were in an uproar.

And Ootah saw why.

A big polar bear

glared down at them.

"Oh, no!" said Ootah.

"Come on, dogs. He is too big."

But the dogs would not listen.

They started toward the bear.

Ootah was afraid that the bear

would kill the dogs.

The dogs leaped at the bear.

The bear swatted them off.

Ootah wanted to throw his harpoon

at the bear.

But he was afraid

that he would kill a dog.

Then Ootah had an idea.

He scrambled up a cliff

behind the bear.

With his knife

he chipped off a piece of ice.

He threw the ice down.

"Oh, please let it work," he said.

The ice hit the bear.

The bear let out a howl.

Then the bear turned

and ran away.

Ootah scrambled down.

The dogs were still barking.

Ootah talked gently to them.

"Good dogs," he said.

"Let's go home."

The sled skimmed across the snow.

Soon they saw the village.

The dogs began to bark.

Ootah began to shout.

"Food! Food for everyone!"

Women and children

ran out of the igloos.

"Food! Food!" they shouted.

Quickly the women cut up the walrus.

They handed out chunks of meat.

Everyone ate the meat.

They ate and they ate.

The dogs ate too.

Soon there was a fire

in every igloo.

There was meat

in every cooking pot.

At night the hunters came back.

They had only a few fish.

They looked sad.

The sleds were empty.

58

The hunters sniffed the air.

"Food!" they shouted.

"Where did it come from?"

"Ootah killed a walrus,"

said Ootah's mother.

"Ootah!" said the hunters.

"Tell us about it," said his father.

Everyone gathered around Ootah,

and he told his story.

Then Ootah's father spoke.
"My son, today you did
a man's work.
Tomorrow you will hunt
with the men."
"Hear! Hear!"
shouted the other hunters.

Ootah could not say a thing.

He was just as happy

as a boy could be.

At last he was a real hunter.